Contents

Tuna Cakes

PREP: 10 min. ■ TOTAL: 26 min. (incl. refrigerating) ■ MAKES: 6 servings.

- **2 cans (5 oz. each) light tuna in water, drained, flaked**
- **1 pkg. (6 oz.) STOVE TOP Stuffing Mix for Chicken**
- **1 cup KRAFT Shredded Mild Cheddar Cheese**
- **³/₄ cup water**
- **1 carrot, shredded**
- **¹/₃ cup KRAFT Real Mayo Mayonnaise**
- **2 Tbsp. CLAUSSEN Sweet Pickle Relish**

COMBINE ingredients. Refrigerate 10 min.

HEAT large nonstick skillet sprayed with cooking spray on medium heat. Use ice cream scoop to add ¹/₃-cup portions of tuna mixture, in batches, to skillet.

FLATTEN into patties with back of spatula. Cook 6 min. or until golden brown on both sides, carefully turning patties over after 3 min.

FOR EASIER HANDLING IN SKILLET:
Mix all ingredients. Shape into patties as directed. Place in single layer on baking sheet. Refrigerate 1 hour before cooking as directed.

STOVE TOP Spinach Balls

PREP: 15 min. ■ TOTAL: 35 min. ■ MAKES: 20 servings.

1 pkg. (6 oz.) STOVE TOP Savory Herbs Stuffing Mix

1²/₃ cups hot water

¼ cup butter or margarine

2 pkg. (10 oz. each) frozen chopped spinach, thawed, well drained and patted dry

1 cup KRAFT Grated Parmesan Cheese

1 cup chopped fresh mushrooms

1 small onion, finely chopped

4 eggs

HEAT oven to 400°F.

MIX stuffing mix, hot water and butter in large bowl until well blended.

ADD remaining ingredients; mix lightly. Shape into 60 (1-inch) balls. Place in single layer in 2 (15×10×1-inch) pans sprayed with cooking spray.

BAKE 15 to 20 min. or until lightly browned.

MAKE AHEAD:
Prepare and bake spinach balls as directed; cool completely. Place in freezer-weight resealable plastic bags; freeze up to 3 months. When ready to serve, thaw in refrigerator. Place on baking sheets and bake at 400°F for 10 to 15 min. or until heated through.

NUTRITION BONUS:
Since these tasty appetizers are rich in vitamin A from the spinach, they can fit into a healthful eating plan. For complete nutritional information, please visit www.kraftrecipes.com.

Easy Party Meatballs

PREP: 10 min. ■ TOTAL: 40 min. ■ MAKES: 24 servings, 2 meatballs each.

1½ **lb. lean ground beef**

1 **pkg. (6 oz.) STOVE TOP Stuffing Mix for Chicken**

⅔ **cup water**

2 **cans (8 oz. each) crushed pineapple, drained**

1 **bottle (18 oz.) KRAFT Original Barbecue Sauce or KRAFT Hickory Smoke Barbecue Sauce**

¼ **cup packed brown sugar**

HEAT oven to 425°F.

MIX meat, stuffing mix and water. Shape into 1-inch balls.

PLACE in 13×9-inch baking dish.

BAKE 20 min. or until done (160°F). Stir in remaining ingredients. Bake 10 min. or until sauce is heated through.

SUBSTITUTE:
Prepare using your favorite KRAFT Barbecue Sauce.

SUBSTITUTE:
Substitute ground chicken or 1½ pkg. (24 oz.) frozen LOUIS RICH Pure Ground Turkey, thawed, for the ground beef.

MAKE AHEAD:
Prepare meatballs as directed. Bake in 425°F oven 20 min. or until done (160°F). Stir in remaining ingredients; cover and refrigerate up to 1 day. To reheat, bake in 425°F oven 20 min. or until meatballs and sauce are heated through.

Spinach-Stuffed Mushrooms

PREP: 15 min. ■ TOTAL: 35 min. ■ MAKES: 40 servings.

1½   **cups hot water**
  1   **pkg. (6 oz.) STOVE TOP Stuffing Mix for Chicken**
 40   **fresh mushrooms (2 lb.)**
  2   **Tbsp. butter**
  2   **cloves garlic, minced**
  1   **pkg. (10 oz.) frozen chopped spinach, thawed, well drained**
  1   **cup KRAFT Shredded Low-Moisture Part-Skim Mozzarella Cheese**
  1   **cup KRAFT Grated Parmesan Cheese**

HEAT oven to 400°F.

ADD hot water to stuffing mix in large bowl; stir just until moistened.

REMOVE stems from mushrooms; chop stems. Melt butter in skillet on medium heat. Add chopped stems and garlic; cook and stir 5 min. or until tender. Add to stuffing with spinach and cheeses; mix well.

SPOON stuffing mixture into mushroom caps. Place, filled sides up, in shallow pan.

BAKE 20 min. or until mushrooms are tender and filling is heated through.

SUBSTITUTE:
Prepare using **STOVE TOP Savory Herbs Stuffing Mix.**

LEFTOVER STUFFING?
Mushrooms vary in size. Any leftover stuffing mixture can be served as a side dish with baked chicken.

Easy Brunch Bake

PREP: 15 min. ■ TOTAL: 55 min. ■ MAKES: 8 servings.

1 **pkg. (6 oz.) STOVE TOP Stuffing Mix for Chicken**

3 **cups fat-free milk**

1 **red pepper, chopped**

1 **pkg. (10 oz.) frozen chopped spinach, thawed, squeezed dry**

1 **cup KRAFT 2% Milk Shredded Sharp Cheddar Cheese**

2 **whole eggs**

2 **egg whites**

4 **slices OSCAR MAYER Bacon, cooked, crumbled**

HEAT oven to 350°F.

COMBINE ingredients.

SPOON into greased 13×9-inch baking dish.

BAKE 40 min. or until center is set and top is golden brown.

MAKE AHEAD:
Assemble recipe as directed. Refrigerate up to 24 hours.
When ready to serve, uncover and bake as directed.

NUTRITION BONUS:
Wow your guests with this tasty, super simple dish that's
packed with nutrition! Not only is the spinach high in vitamin
A, but the red pepper is a good source of vitamin C and the
cheese provides calcium. For complete nutritional
information, please visit www.kraftrecipes.com.

STOVE TOP Spinach & Feta Stuffin' Egg Muffin

PREP: 15 min. ■ TOTAL: 40 min. ■ MAKES: 6 servings.

1 pkg. (6 oz.) STOVE TOP Stuffing Mix for Chicken

1 pkg. (10 oz.) chopped frozen spinach, drained

7 eggs

½ cup crumbled ATHENOS Feta Cheese with Basil & Tomato

HEAT oven to 400°F.

PREPARE stuffing as directed on package; cool 5 min.

PRESS ¼ cup stuffing onto bottom and up side of each of 12 muffin cups sprayed with cooking spray, forming ¼-inch rim around top of each; fill with spinach.

BEAT eggs in measuring cup; pour over stuffing cups. Top with cheese.

BAKE 20 min. or until centers are set. Let stand 5 min. before serving.

HOW TO EASILY REMOVE MUFFINS:
Run knife around edges of the baked muffin cups to make it easier to remove them from the muffin pan.

SERVING SUGGESTION:
Serve with fresh fruit to round out the meal.

Ham and Cheese Stuff 'n Puff

PREP: 5 min. ■ TOTAL: 1 hour 10 min. ■ MAKES: 6 servings.

5 eggs

1 cup milk

½ cup BREAKSTONE'S or KNUDSEN Sour Cream

1 pkg. (10 oz.) frozen chopped broccoli, thawed, drained

1 pkg. (6 oz.) STOVE TOP Stuffing Mix for Chicken

1½ pkg. (6 oz. each) OSCAR MAYER Smoked Ham, chopped

1 cup KRAFT Shredded Cheddar Cheese, divided

HEAT oven to 375°F.

BEAT eggs, milk and sour cream in large bowl with whisk until well blended. Add broccoli, stuffing mix, ham and ½ cup cheese; mix lightly.

POUR into 2-qt. casserole; cover loosely with foil.

BAKE 1 hour. Uncover. Sprinkle with remaining cheese; bake 5 min. or until cheese is melted and broccoli mixture is heated through.

SUBSTITUTE:
Use whatever frozen vegetables and shredded cheese you have on hand, such as peas and KRAFT Shredded Mozzarella Cheese.

Pork Chops with Apples and Stuffing

PREP: 10 min. ■ TOTAL: 50 min. ■ MAKES: 6 servings.

1 pkg. (6 oz.) STOVE TOP Stuffing Mix for Chicken

1 can (21 oz.) apple pie filling

6 boneless pork loin chops (1½ lb.), ¾-inch thick

HEAT oven to 375°F.

PREPARE stuffing as directed on package.

SPREAD pie filling onto bottom of 13×9-inch baking dish sprayed with cooking spray; top with chops and stuffing. Cover with foil.

BAKE 40 min. or until chops are done (145°F), removing foil after 30 min.

SUBSTITUTE:
Prepare using 6 boneless skinless chicken breasts.

SPECIAL EXTRA:
Certain flavors go extremely well with pork. So if you want to pair pork chops or a roast with the perfect ingredients, try these suggestions: thyme, sage, bay leaves, garlic, mustard, apples, prunes, pineapple and sauerkraut.

Stuffing-Topped Beef Filets

PREP: 10 min. ■ TOTAL: 27 min. ■ MAKES: 2 servings.

2 beef tenderloin filets (½ lb.)

1 Tbsp. butter

½ cup shredded zucchini

⅓ cup finely chopped onions

¾ cup STOVE TOP Stuffing Mix for Chicken in the Canister

½ cup KRAFT Shredded Cheddar Cheese

HEAT broiler.

HEAT ovenproof skillet on medium heat. Add meat; cook 6 min. on each side or until medium doneness. Remove from skillet; cover to keep warm.

MELT butter in same skillet on medium-high heat. Add zucchini and onions; cook and stir 2 min. or until crisp-tender. Transfer to large bowl; stir in stuffing mix and cheese. Add meat to skillet; top with stuffing mixture.

BROIL, 6 inches from heat source, 5 min. or until stuffing is lightly browned.

SERVING SUGGESTION:
Serve with a crisp mixed green salad tossed with your favorite KRAFT Light Dressing.

SUBSTITUTE:
If you are a blue cheese lover, substitute ¼ cup ATHENOS Crumbled Blue Cheese for the ½ cup Cheddar.

STOVE TOP Sweet Citrus Chicken

PREP: 10 min. ■ TOTAL: 40 min. ■ MAKES: 6 servings.

1²/₃ cups hot water

1 pkg. (6 oz.) STOVE TOP Stuffing Mix for Chicken

6 small boneless skinless chicken breasts (1¹/₂ lb.), pounded to ¹/₂-inch thickness

²/₃ cup orange juice

¹/₃ cup packed brown sugar

3 Tbsp. butter or margarine, melted

HEAT oven to 400°F.

ADD hot water to stuffing mix; stir just until moistened.

PLACE chicken in 13×9-inch baking dish. Mix juice, sugar and butter until blended; pour over chicken. Top with stuffing.

BAKE 30 min. or until chicken is done (165°F).

SUBSTITUTE:
Substitute honey for the brown sugar.

Cheesy Chicken & Broccoli Bake

PREP: 10 min. ■ TOTAL: 50 min. ■ MAKES: 6 servings.

1 pkg. (6 oz.) STOVE TOP Stuffing Mix for Chicken

1½ lb. boneless skinless chicken breasts, cut into bite-size pieces

1 pkg. (16 oz.) frozen broccoli florets, thawed, drained

1 can (10¾ oz.) reduced-sodium condensed cream of chicken soup

½ lb. (8 oz.) VELVEETA Pasteurized Prepared Cheese Product, cut into ½-inch cubes

HEAT oven to 400°F.

PREPARE stuffing as directed on package; set aside.

COMBINE remaining ingredients; spoon into 13×9-inch baking dish. Top with stuffing.

BAKE 40 min. or until chicken is done (165°F).

Dressed-Up Fish Rolls for a Crowd

PREP: 10 min. ■ TOTAL: 35 min. ■ MAKES: 10 servings.

1 pkg. (6 oz.) STOVE TOP Cornbread Stuffing Mix

¾ cup KRAFT Zesty Italian Dressing

¼ cup chopped fresh parsley

½ tsp. garlic powder

¼ tsp. paprika

10 whitefish fillets (2½ lb.)

HEAT oven to 425°F.

PREPARE stuffing as directed on package. Mix next 4 ingredients until well blended; brush half onto fish.

SPOON stuffing onto one end of each fish fillet; roll up. Place, seam-sides down, in 13×9-inch baking dish sprayed with cooking spray. Top with remaining dressing mixture.

BAKE 20 to 25 min. or until fish flakes easily with fork.

COOKING KNOW HOW:
For best results, use thin flounder or sole fillets.

Cheesy Green Bean Casserole

PREP: 10 min. ▪ TOTAL: 40 min. ▪ MAKES: 14 servings.

2 bags (16 oz. each) frozen French cut green beans, thawed

1 can (10¾ oz.) condensed cream of mushroom soup

1 cup CHEEZ WHIZ Cheese Dip

1½ cups hot water

¼ cup margarine

1 pkg. (6 oz.) STOVE TOP Stuffing Mix for Chicken

HEAT oven to 350°F.

COMBINE beans, soup and CHEEZ WHIZ in 2-qt. casserole.

ADD hot water to margarine in medium bowl; stir until melted. Stir in stuffing mix just until moistened. Spoon over bean mixture.

BAKE 30 min. or until heated through.

MAKE AHEAD:
Assemble casserole as directed. Refrigerate up to 24 hours. When ready to serve, bake, uncovered, at 350°F for 45 to 50 min. or until heated through.

Stuffing-Topped Vegetable Bake

PREP: 25 min. ■ TOTAL: 45 min. ■ MAKES: 10 servings, ¾ cup each.

- **4 cups broccoli florets**
- **4 cups cauliflower florets**
- **1 tub (10 oz.) PHILADELPHIA Savory Garlic Cooking Creme**
- **1 cup KRAFT Shredded Triple Cheddar Cheese with a TOUCH OF PHILADELPHIA**
- **1 pkg. (6 oz.) STOVE TOP Stuffing Mix for Chicken**

HEAT oven to 375°F.

COOK vegetables in boiling water in medium saucepan 3 min.; drain well. Return vegetables to pan. Add cooking creme; toss to coat. Spoon into 13×9-inch baking dish sprayed with cooking spray; top with Cheddar.

PREPARE stuffing as directed on package; spoon over vegetable mixture.

BAKE 20 min. or until heated through. Let stand 5 min. before serving.

SERVING SUGGESTION:
This vegetable side dish makes a great accompaniment to a serving of lean meat or poultry.

FOOD FACTS:
For best results, both the broccoli and cauliflower florets should be the same size, about 2 inches, so they cook evenly.